draw me without boundaries

Margaret Gibson

draw

me

without

boundaries

LOUISIANA STATE UNIVERSITY PRESS

BATON ROUGE

Published by Louisiana State University Press
lsupress.org

LSU Press Paperback Original

Designer: Michelle A. Neustrom
Typeface: Calluna

Cover illustration: *The Spiral Path,* by Pamela Zagarenski, 2022

LIBRARY OF CONGRESS CATALOGING-IN-PUBLICATION DATA

Names: Gibson, Margaret, 1944– author.
Title: Draw me without boundaries / Margaret Gibson.
Description: Baton Rouge : Louisiana State University Press, 2024. | LSU Press
    paperback original.
Identifiers: LCCN 2024001029 (print) | LCCN 2024001030 (ebook) |
    ISBN 978-0-8071-8245-1 (paperback) | ISBN 978-0-8071-8267-3 (epub) |
    ISBN 978-0-8071-8268-0 (pdf)
Subjects: LCGFT: Poetry. | Monologues (Drama)
Classification: LCC PS3557.I1916 D73 2024 (print) | LCC PS3557.I1916 (ebook) |
    DDC 811/.54—dc23/eng/20240402
LC record available at https://lccn.loc.gov/2024001029
LC ebook record available at https://lccn.loc.gov/2024001030

This body is not me; I am not caught in this body, I am life without boundaries, I have never been born and I have never died . . . Since beginningless time I have always been free. Birth and death are only a door through which we go in and out.

—THICH NHAT HANH

draw me without boundaries

LENA

Around my body there is light the color of daybreak on a day it will rain.

The light is also the color of the roses she grew in her summer garden, roses she put into vases
                        along a narrow strip of mirror on a polished table.

Roses above; roses below.

Doubled blooming—was that what I called it?

She is looking inside, as one might rummage in a drawer. Where the memories are, there also are words.
                        She must have put them somewhere.

She hears the rattle of the breakfast cart.

The day begins.

There's a tidal river outside her window. There's a river in her wrist.

Once there was a field. It overlooked a river hidden by trees, green in the distance—
I could find the early morning river
                        by the twists and turns of the mist

that lifted over the trees and into the air.

Now that's how I live—in and out of the twists and turns of mist
and in bursts of light.

Where does it go? The morning, the mist, the river, the field?

She has been brought to a place where men and women have wheels.

Where she is called "my little friend" right before someone holds her wrists
and another pair of hands takes down her slacks

and wipes her bottom with a towel. She has no say in the matter.

Just coming into the room now, a woman-shadow with a low voice
asks questions she can't quite hear.

*Like a distant rumble, that voice—as in a field with a ridge of trees
against a sky before storm.*

Black, green, yellow. She sees them as bands of color.

Black for sky, green for trees along a ridge, yellow for the field—

*Let me speak, let me speak now: the field must be new flowering
with mustard and goldfinch. That's why it's yellow.*

Il n'y a personne dans le champ. There is no one in the field.

*Yes, I speak French. My granddaughter, also. It was our private language
in the family, years ago.*

I talk to myself now, missing missing missing her.

She nods her head when the woman-shadow offers toast with jam,
a cup of tea.

"I am an elegant peasant," she says aloud.

My husband said so, she thinks, and nods again. *Mais oui.*

The day before they brought her to this place, she jumped into the pond
back home,
         and that leap—so glorious—

surprised her stepchildren, huddled inside making plans, no idea that she was
now
    a naked woman

loping across the grass, pitching her shirt into the cattails, and in one continuous
arising,
       as if she were a great blue heron

finally lifting over the weeds and silt and frogs' eggs and lily pads . . .

*Yes, and I landed in the deep brown water, smack into a spring, an underwater
uprush so icy*
        I yelped liked a wild thing.

They said she'd wandered away, confused. Surely, she hadn't heard them
in the house,
         in the next room, surely

she hadn't heard them talking about what to take, and the clothes she'd need.

They were doing what they thought best. They were doing what they thought
    they had to.

Or so they said they said they said.

When I pray, I whisper. I can hear myself.

I'm not as deaf as I make out to be.

There's a tidal river outside her window. There is a river in her wrist.

Each day, to overcome her resistance to being fully present in this place,
she baits a hook.

Morning mist has erased the horizon line between river and sky, erased form,
erased all color but this

opalescent shimmer
                    into which rows a human form in a low-slung boat.

Heart pump, an ache in the arm muscles, steady breath, and the wake widens
    behind the small boat,

the wake, the wake, the wake

Now she can study the man in the boat, right down to the stripes in the plaid
    of his wool jacket,

which reeks of fish and bait and sweat,

and she will never know this man who crosses her window, skimming into her
    awareness, stirring up words,
                    making her pulse go a little faster.

A prayer I am trying to remember ends with ends with ends with . . .

She drops a line into the river, and she waits.

Afterwards, they said she'd wandered away from the house, confused.

Would it be like an auction, sold to the highest bidder?
Realtors. Scavengers.

Yes, yes, but also there was a field. There were woods. There was sky. And a river.

She listened to them talking. She looked up at the sky and wept.

Pray for the field. The woods. The river. The pond,
and yes,
            pray for the garden, the garden, the garden . . .

I took off my clothes in the garden. Not
all of them, no. There was his old blue shirt,
I still had that on, the work shirt I'd later
toss into the cattails after I'd taken off
all my clothes. I broke stems of earth fragrance
and rubbed the leaves between my hands,
basil and rosemary and sage, he had been gone
from the house for years, my late, my late,
my late one, your grandfather, he had been gone
looking for his memory, losing his words, it was
a bone in my throat, that loneliness, no—not
a bone, a thought like a bone: You will, always
now, be here alone, said the bone, and I worked
in the garden because I couldn't speak. I worked
until the daisies and the phlox stooped over
in the afternoon heat, then off went shoes,
off trousers, pants, shirt, bra, and I rubbed
dirt, garden dirt, onto my breasts and belly,
I smeared it—what on earth was I thinking?
and when I put on the shirt—that's right,
his blue work shirt—I was completely calm,
no one could see me, the yard is surrounded by

woods, I could take my time, and I took it, I was
myself again all the way down to the cattails
and water skimmers, blue dragonflies skating
on the overhead white clouds, the clouds doubled
onto the surface of the water, it's all about mirrors,
the mind. I don't know how long I stood there
looking into the pond, then I plunged in.
Whole body in, and that's how it happened.
All the years with my husband in the woods,
in the field, in the pond, still surface or ruffled,
rosemary basil sage, each time we touched
or laughed or were sullen or mad as hornets,
each time we made plans, made bad puns,
made love, or tried to help the other understand
what couldn't be understood, and I got my life back,
one leap, doubled, we used to leap into it together,
we'd swim, we made love in the spillway, yes,
all of it came back came back came back,
all of it . . . Mais j'etais toujours seule . . .
But I was still alone . . .

And then she heard them, calling her name, crying out, running toward her.

There is a drawing, framed and on the wall in her room, just inside, by the door.

She likes to stop and look at it, ignoring the aide at her side who worries
that standing too long in one spot will tire her.

She draws the drawing into herself, she lets it drop down into the depths
of her solitude

as she looks at the snow fields on both sides of a road whose borders are softened
by drifts of snow,
                    and the road,

the road seems to flow beyond the limits of her vision, more river than road.

Zoe drew it, the road that flows. Zoe Zoe Zoe. She was just thirteen.

Standing there, she is grateful to have come this far. Given her age, she has lived,
and she knows it,

nearly all the life she's been given to live, whether she dies tomorrow or next year.

And she is grateful. Grateful, and also . . . well, yes. *Merci.* It's still there. *Regret.*

Gratitude and regret. She regards them as if they are snow.

"Well now, she says." *Each one, a flake of snow.*

I have been brought to a place where men and women have wheels.

Where a nurse-girl puts plastic beads around her neck and asks
what she liked to cook for Thanksgiving.
"What's your favorite pie?"

If you're a man, the nurse-girl says, "Can you believe it, he was a physicist."
Or a professor. Or a capitalist:
"He used to own this town."

It doesn't much matter if you obey or rebel, if you are wealthy, ugly, sexy,
downtrodden, or own your own house.

Anyone may end up here with no say in the matter.

One afternoon a woman-shadow takes a book from her bookshelf, turns the
pages, turns to her and asks,

"Did you write this, Lena?"
She smiled then. "Yes, I did."

She smiles now as she watches her fingers moving across the bed table.

If she could find the words the words the words, she could have her say.

She's typing words words words. The silence is filled with words.

I am thinking with my fingers, she thinks.

And yes, here they are, finally my fingers find the closing words of the prayer
I've been waiting for:
"awakening the heart from its ancient sleep."

ZOE

As soon as I knew I would live by myself, I sold out. I took the paintings I considered my best work, the work I loved, the work that had dreamed itself through me more deeply than any lover, and I said to the head of the gallery: *Sell.* I didn't bother to change from my paint-pants to the one pair of linen trousers I own. I walked the twenty blocks to my gallery and said to the owner, "Okay, you win. Sell them for as much as you can." Sell them, hard line and soft, collage and watercolor shimmer. Sell my dream of the sea. Sell my dream of the sea whose power is boundless. Sell the sea. Too much has changed. I give up. I give it up, I give it back—the sea's too full, rushing with tidal force, with tsunami force, a great wave unrolling, no choice left, no safety, no rescue, no excuse, no refuge but going into the seethe and rush of the sea's pouring over the edge of the boundless, all this in the sound of my letting my breath out slow, all this when I knew I would leave the city and live by myself.

There was a time when paintings were made for people. A time when art was communal, when it was sacred, when it was public. There was a time when ordinary men and women of limited means could buy art for their own walls and live within the color of art and with its images or absence of image until the art lived in them as close as impulse, as potent as dream. Not now. The gallery owner says,

"You live where you live, you do what you have to."
Before this I'd instructed him not to price the paintings so steeply an ordinary man or woman couldn't buy it. I'd sworn: no sales to fortress art, not a dime to the collectors who buy art as an investment, send it to a secured vault and wait, wait, wait until somewhere the money ripens, the investment proves sound, the buyer sells a painting he's never seen, never lived with, never let pass through his own mind or heart. From one fortress to another the painting goes. I couldn't do it; I just couldn't. I can think of no better mockery of what it is to be human than to sell what has been part of you, too intimate to be said. An intimacy that can only be shown to you in silence or in a dream, so intimate it only emerges, line by line by color by tatter of seaweed . . . Leaving the city, I bow to the sea, driving along a diminished New England coast. I know where I must go, who I must see.

And I bow once again to the sea as I push open the door to Room 19. Amma is in bed, in her purple bathrobe, her silver hair tied behind with a blue ribbon. The tray table is across the bed and, propped up by pillows and the tilt of the bed, Amma is tapping on the tray table as one would on a laptop. Tapping, tapping intently. She does not hear me, doesn't look up. I take a moment to remember Amma's long hands, dirt under the nails, the palms square, her fingers shorter than they should be for a well-proportioned hand. She kept the nails trimmed close. Her hands now seem smaller; everything about her is smaller, but the light in her eyes—now she has looked up, now she has seen me—has not diminished. Immediately, in her eyes a flash of light, she knows now that the silhouette standing in the light of the open door is me. "Let me look at you," she says. And we hold hands, we look at each other quietly. *People don't take each other in,* Amma used to complain. *They should just keep still in that first moment of seeing each other.* And it's true. Silence gets you under each other's skin. Mark used to love that about me. I swallow his name before it takes me away from noticing that Amma's brown eyes are rimmed with blue—the blue of distance and horizon, contemplative blue, tidal blue, depth-charge blue. The sea-change blue of a memory made irretrievable, the pathways to it obscured. Chiaroscuro blue, as she tells me she's been writing to me every day. She seems to think I know the words she has written. I feel a blue thrill of dismay—the moment has depths I hadn't sensed. It is like walking out into the sea on a long sandbar, suddenly slipping over the edge of all attachment, feeling it in your feet, the loss of contact with the ground, floating into depth, remembering to breathe as everything, everything begins dissolving into not-knowing and the subtle force of flow and undertow becomes a blur of blue in the mind, and you are immersed in distance and lostness.

In her guise of a diminished old woman, Amma doesn't fool me. I sense that a door has flung open "inside" her, and she wanders there, inside herself looking and asking, asking and longing. And almost I turn, almost I close the door, almost I vanish. Too much is changing. My marriage. My work. My life. I stare at the bookcase, flush with longing for what I can no longer see, what I can no longer touch. Longing—longing only gets you into trouble. I hate the distance in the word—so I move a chair to the side of the bed and sit, stroking her arm. Amma's right here. She smiles and reaches over with her other arm and touches my lower lip with her thumb. With this small gesture she lets me know that she senses something I don't know—always I have that feeling about her. But I don't ask questions. We look out the window together at the river. There is sunlight on the water, sunlight on the grass. Not a gentle light—it's brash, a color green mixed with yellow so strident you'd think, were the color on canvas, it's unnatural. And yet how natural it feels to sit here with Amma. It makes me feel come home . . .

home when I hadn't planned
to come here first, and yet: all morning, Amma's voice was nesting in my ear,
the way the sound of the sea spirals inside a conch. When I think of Amma,
I think of sitting out with her on the grass in the big chairs Grampa had loved.
We were nowhere near the sea, or so I thought, but she called the light wind
in the oaks a sea breeze. I thought she meant the wind was *like* the low green
evening light birds sweep through, a light that is close to the color of the sunlit
sea. But no. She said that the wind from the Sound, on certain evenings, travels
over Mystic and Old Mystic, over the feed corn and dust of Ledyard, over the
stone walls of North Stonington, through second growth forest: wind that
retains the smell of salt and kelp, wind that carries the sea, beckoning—

and how far inland the sea has expanded now, beyond its old borders and tide lines. I read about climate emergency, but I can also see it unfolding at my feet. Since The Warming, there have been great waves and into human settlements and cities a tidal influx, acidic infusions, broken shells mingled with older glacial till and with the fractured shells of the last of the barnacles and keel worms, with sea snail and mussel shells, and, far from here, the corals blanched white as a dead man's knuckles. The sea now polymer and plastic. Many summers ago, as Amma spoke, I began to smell the sea—that is, the sea as it used to be. I let it pour through me. Each day, before anything else, I used to bow as I dipped my brush into the memory of the sea as I approached bare canvas, where Amma's pervasive invasive pensive ocean stirs, then rushes through me.

And I did not—when I knew I would live entirely by myself, when I knew I would leave a marriage that was no longer a marriage, when I knew I would sell everything and leave—I did not know I would come to the edge of the sea inside myself and stand there, tasting my aloneness in the company of Amma's inner solitude. And yet, here I am, loving the sea that was and the sea that, ruined, isn't itself anymore. Loving my life as it was and now isn't. Wondering what else I can't imagine will, or will have to, happen.

LENA

Well now.

Out the window the light has changed and the river with it.

She retreats inside herself; she retreats into Room 19.

She is thinking with her fingers.

And then, at last, Zoe!

Zoe Zoe Zoe! Oh, my dear one, you have come.

And yet Zoe isn't looking at her. She approaches the bed, but then she stops.

She is looking at the bookcase.

She is asking the bookcase a question.
                                        "How could he?"

That's what she whispers. She shades into a shadow of herself.

Now the Zoe-shadow grows more silent, the one propped up in bed, smaller.

*Dear one, dear Zoe. And so: you have discovered that even marriage
is no solution for loneliness.*

Et qu'il peut aussi inclure la tromperie. And that it may also include deception.

ZOE

Watching Amma watch me, I remember how stubborn she is. How she wouldn't consent to letting them move her here unless she be given Grampa's old room. That's completely unreasonable, my mother said. I insist, said Amma, and she quoted an old Zen poem. "No snowflake falls in the wrong place," she said. She said she liked the number 19. "I feel 19," she insisted, "but my knees feel 150. It averages out about right." My mother secured the room, brought her books and photographs, the little bookcase, the Bose, and the CD of Russian choral music and Japanese flutes— and the blues. "To match the puddle in my heart," Amma said. And she wanted books. "You haven't written for years—be sensible." And then my mother softened. "I think it's beautiful you're still wanting to be close to Dad, after all these years." Amma nodded, closing her eyes. "Thank you. I'm so tired of being lonely." When Amma was brought here, she gave me a ring Grampa had given her on their 40th anniversary, opals that resemble the winter sky, blue and gray, but in a change of light, the stones flash fire. Just like Amma. Every day I wear her ring, except when I paint.

LENA

You have been here to see me.

*You were once a baby. You were a baby with cheeks so full
they drooped.*

*When you were small, I'd carry you in my arms, I'd sing
the little Zoe lullaby song—*

I still sing it to myself, whenever I can remember it.

*On the table by an east window at home
there was a blown-glass globe
the color of the sea
as a wave rises and the sun
shines through the cresting,*

*and how could you mind, it is so beautiful being dashed on the shore,
sometimes we come ashore*
                    dashed into tatters and syllables—

*Oh, my dear one when you were a baby
I would hold you
and we would float together
in the light of the sea
cresting into the air, I could
hold us both up . . .*

You have been here.

Afterwards, she ate an egg and mashed potatoes for supper. Then she slept.

Somewhere inside, there are words, and an ocean, and the sea-light of a woman
who said,
        "Amma, my socks have salt water in them. They're still damp—
            I have the ocean in my socks."

La mer s'est rapprochée du soleil. The sea has moved closer. The sea has moved closer to the sun.

Je sais que tu fais encore l'amour avec lui.

I know that you still make love with him.

I saw it in the curve of your lower lip.

ZOE

                                                When I knew I would
live by myself, I went to the sea, and I stood at the edge of it. On edge. I had
thought that to stand beside the ruined sea, so completely alone, would offer
me a lesson in assent. I thought I could see the ocean paint itself, broken
line by broken line, the water angled into waves and roiling. I thought my
heart, constricted and hardened, would soften, open. When I knew I would
live by myself, I went to the sea. There, I thought, I can imagine a future that
might have been, not the one I have now, altered beyond my expectations. Or
perhaps I wanted to imagine a future in which I taste aloneness without being
frightened—but what I found was . . .

cradle and memory, salt light and family shadow. Sandwiches with sand in them. Sand turrets that slump into the sea. What is being in a family but a lesson in shaping and shapeshifting? In a way, it is standing at the edge of the sea, with mist for horizon, sea wrack at your feet. Each wave crests, breaks, withdraws, and begins again, leaving behind it sea glass, the sharp edges sanded off. Here's the sea glass I'm left to gather and keep as my own. From my father, steadiness; from my mother, laughter, tenacity, courage, and a mighty will. From Grampa, I learned sea mist and April snow. Nothing lasts. From Amma, oh from Amma, how to keep my eye on the horizon and to cross over it if necessary; to shift as the light shifts. And to look beyond line and light. To stand in silence, without any idea of what I'm looking for.

Beyond line and light, I remember
Amma and Grampa sitting together on the seawall at Watch Hill. They sat
leaning into each other, facing the sea, arms loosely around each other, their
backs to the camera and to the rest of us there with them. They sat in their
aloneness together, between their bodies a keyhole of space in which I could
glimpse the sea; between their bodies a fissure through which—unasked,
unimaginable, unowned—there glinted the devastations of love.

The devastations of love . . . Am I listening to myself? Do I hear myself? When I went back to the seawall at Watch Hill, I listened only to the gulls. To the wind. To the stillness of the light in which I saw first Mark's shadow, next his silhouette, and only then his body. Rather, his body as a Greek torso of Apollo. Without arms. Marble. The marble discolored and pitted from having been on the floor of the ocean for centuries. "I am in love with someone else," he said, "but I don't want to lose you." *Both/and,* he said, his voice coming out of a noble head, hair in stylized curls, the gaze turned slightly away. A god never looks directly into your eyes. A god is incapable of being faithful.

We first made love at the lip of low tide. We were married on sand, above the tide line, under a red tent with streamers of gold flowing away into the wind. Fixed and flowing. Body is archipelago, sea water and space, through which we reach over to someone else. A momentary . . . solidity. We were married on sand, looking into a sea of light— tidal, willing to be whelmed. And so, when Mark asked me to meet him beside the sea I said yes. His voice was like a seabird down-rolling on a thermal. And I said, holding my ground, imposing a condition, "Yes, I will meet you, but only at Watch Hill." Before I leave for good. At the lip of low tide one more time, even in this late winter chill. Your body, my body fixed and flowing into a now-altered and overwhelming ocean of regret and desire.

After, when I knew, now without any doubt, that I would live by myself, forsaking all others, I turned my back on the sea. I left the city, stopping to see Amma, stopping to see my mother and father, to let them know that I'm staying at Amma's old house to paint. An uninterrupted time to paint. Just to paint, I said. Then inland to Amma's house, which is sitting empty, if absence of human voice and word is emptiness. The house is old, over three-hundred years old. Once it lay near ruin, a wild thing, a den, a refuge, a burrow. Over time, its various owners each staged a comeback . . . a rebirth. Now no one in the family needs it; money is needed, but the house hasn't sold. Off market, it gathers silence and dust and a feathering of vine up the back patio wall, a fringe of moss and lichen on the north-facing cedar shake shingles. Like me, the house is letting go, forsaking all others.

Forsaking all others, I work with what I see. And from where I stand. I stand outside Amma's house, in an inland sea of trees. Are there fewer trees? The oaks, for instance, still here but skeletal, having yielded to successive infestations and drought. They look like driftwood. And the maples? How can I count what's *missing?* I've lost count. Almost I can hear, as if outside of myself, a sigh of relief. *Nothing stays,* the house reminds me. The seasons are all mixed up. As the wind lifts and changes direction, I watch an early morning shadow of the dogwood sketch itself onto the white clapboards. The house is its drawing pad. Now, when I go inside, I feel the house close over me as if I have entered the sea itself. In the hallway, I feel the pull of the tides. I let my breath out slow. Surrender has the taste of salt. Now I know that I am subject to birth, growth, separation, loneliness, sickness, sorrow, death, and lamentation. As for renewal, there is only the going on and the getting over.

LENA

You have been here to see me,
your eyes shining.

You have been here.

You looked and looked. At me.
At the river the river the river
flowing slowly east to the sea.

Now you are not here. Where did you go?

Tu n'es pas avec moi. You are not with me.

When you return, perhaps
the moment will
expand and expand

until past and future
collapse into
what is endlessly present.

The way forward is the way back.

Je pense que tu es l'enfant je n'ai jamais eu.

I think you are the child I never had.

ZOE

How long have I been here? In this house, in this body? I have counted the days over and over and over: sufficient. I have taken the tests, over and over, my hands shaking. *Positive.* Positive? The timing is awful. My body has betrayed me. First, with its desire. His body, my body, fixed and flowing at the edge of the sea—where on impulse, on impulse, I thought, *How could it hurt, how could it matter?*

It hurts, it matters.
So many years of trying. We wore ourselves out, trying. I thought I was impregnable. He built houses by the sea; I painted the sea. I housed my paintings on the walls he raised. Sometimes the houses opened and let the sea inside, let The Warming inside. I must be a house. Did I not open, did I not let the sea inside? He took me, standing up and beside the sea. He put the sea inside me, just when I thought I had turned my back on it. Sell, I said to my agent. Just when I thought I was done, when I thought I was safe and entirely on my own . . . my body, it's betrayed me.

INTERVALE

The Earth continues.

Ice calves into the sea in sheets from the ice cliffs in Antarctica and Greenland. A coral reef in the Pacific whitens.

In New Orleans, the cleanup from the last hurricane drags on. In Oregon and California, ash from the forest fires has tainted the grapes in the vineyards.

The Earth continues.

In New York, a family moves into a basement one-room apartment—affordable, but too small—without knowing that in five years one of them will drown in that room during an offshore nor'easter's steady gales of flood-rain and wind.

A river between two countries and the low-lying land along the winding river is considered an inadequate boundary, and the talk of funding a steep wall to keep out immigrants continues.

The Earth continues,

leafing out in some places, drying out in others. Fewer birds return to North American forests, the stock market shudders and shrinks, oil companies continue to drill and frack and pipe and ignore the common life. The stock market surges.

Then COVID, or SARS-CoV-2, surges.

LENA

This is what I hear:

Go to your room.
                        Stay away from others.

Wear masks.

Where did everybody go?

Can you see us behind the shut doors to our rooms? Can. you see us behind our masks?

The tide that has washed the inhabitants of Chestnut Cottage from the shoreline and into the depths of their single rooms

has stranded the residents within the common life of the dementia wing.

Just look at us.

Yvette, who weeps.

Marion, who at ninety-seven has the blue eyes of a child on her birthday.

Jim, who used to clear his throat in an avalanche of noise only when his wife was present for the half hour she sat with him at lunch.

Bob, who wept with joy when someone's granddaughter, her hair in a blonde braid, sat down and played the out-of-tune piano in the common room, and Beethoven's moonlight quavered into the common air.

Graham, who escaped out the exit door without the alarm sounding—how did he do that? Then spent an entire half hour by himself in the garden.

Mama, who is wide as the piano and salty as lasagna.

Betty, an only child, who has no children, and who always puts herself first. She likes being in her room alone.

Gurden, who, only wanting to be kissed, has become humanity's harshest critic.

Jessie, who once took a long cigar-shaped cookie between her fingers, put it to her lips, winked, and pretended to inhale.

And Lena, who is thinking with her fingers.

Where did everyone go?

I will be ready to listen if you come. When you come.

Zoe Zoe Zoe.

I hold a space within me in which you may reappear. Je garde en moi un espace . . .

I am in Room 19.

I AM Room 19.

Room 19 becomes a world. The fragment becomes the whole.

This is called enlightenment.

"You have good days and bad days." *That's what the woman-shadow tells me . . .*
The lower half of her face is missing.

I don't know who she thinks I am, and I don't know who she is.

She moves a white wet cloth, like an eraser, over my arms and hands.

Beyond the window, my words are silent leaves on a flow-down river-down . . .

Down down down . . .

There you go. *That's what the woman-shadow says.*

I want "Here you are." She says, "There you go," feeding me a spoonful
of soft, hot
                something or other.

The river says it, too. There there there you go.

The woman-shadow pauses and watches her tapping on the bedsheets, her
    hands moving

as if on a keyboard.

"I am writing blank verse." *That's what I said.*

Ha, Ha!

I have a granddaughter.
                    Don't I have a granddaughter?

So I must have had children.
                    Did I have children?

My husband had children.
                    (That was lucky.)

So I had step-children. And then grandchildren, and so . . .

I have a granddaughter, but they won't let me let me let me

see her,
            let me see her . . .

When the door closes, in the silence of Room 19, her fingers fall silent.

J'ai oblié qui je suis. I have forgotten who I am.

She stares at the bookcase. She watches the river:

Have I forgotten?
        Who says so?
                Who is this "I" who says so?

She drifts into the drawing on the wall, down the road that is more river than
road.

Today I am having a good day, I can tell tell tell.

Today I know this:

one afternoon, long before his illness,
I brought him a glass of water,
and he drank it, sitting there
on the stone wall he was working on.
He drank it down, all of it, as if it were
his life, my life, life itself.

He drank it down.

"Already I can see it, the wall,
once it's finished—
how it fits this space, how it
curves, runs, turns, completes itself.
The work now is this stone,
this one, particular
and heavy,
    then this next one,
then that one,
the one with a mica haze
and evening sky in its surface.
A beauty—if it fits."

Then he looked at me.
      "You're a beauty,

Lena Rivers," he said, and handed me
the glass,
   empty of water, full of sunlight.

ZOE

A time to live and a time to die . . . but this is no time to have a child. *To have a child is personal. To have a child is also . . . political.* Amma wrote that in a journal, and I tore the page out and taped it to my easel in her old study. I don't consult my mother because I know what she'd want me to do. She'd have advice. Amma would say, "Wait and see . . . go slow." *Go slow.* I practice walking on the uneven boards of this old house. I listen to the silence. I live now in a house that has no phone hooked up, no Wifi. No zoom. *Go slow.* I bathe in the pond, I dry off in the sun. I go into the house and before blank drawing paper, I wait. The image that comes unbidden is charred, impossibly limping home, afraid to drink water or seek food, everything is tainted, everything is radioactive. Then a child: perfect to the eye, a child who smells of rice and milk, but whose DNA no longer has a will of its own, whose invisible organs are programed now to convulse and crumple, whose skin blooms a rash of roses, whose mind knows only pain. And so, yes:

there is a time to live,
a time to die—and in this, my allotted time in history, sheltering in place,
with thousands beginning to sicken from COVID and die, who would want
to bring a child into viral ignorance and denial, into polar slosh and forest
die-off, into tidal devastations, into a time of collapse and extinction? Who
would choose *now,* when even I, on a perfect blue-sky day, have seen a skein of
geese plummet from the sky over a coastal marsh? Nothing visible to fault or
blame. And no sound. Although there was an odd smell from the wetland. Who
would choose now to be born, when so many (not Amma, not yet) are dying in
hospitals, on ventilators, dying alone—

dying in a time when very few have the ears of the Bodhisattva, who, it is said, hears the cries of those who are in pain. Do I have the many arms and hands of She who lulls and rocks and soothes and wipes away the tears of those who suffer? Why would I want a child now? I can't take care of a child. I'm alone. Alone—and I protest my aloneness, even if I choose it. Even if I choose it, I refuse to embrace it. Oh, I did, for a time, paint signs, and I held them up. Against nukes, against poverty, against war. I painted my face, I painted signs, I marched with others, many times. But there is now no holding up of signs, no vigils, no marches, no time with others. There is I, just I, thousands of us restricted to "just I," making a retreat into the personal, away from a life with others.

Waking up, watching the light deepen in the room, I would sometimes realize, "I am an artist," as if I was confessing to happiness— if one can be happy in a time when children are gunned down at school and geese fall from the sky. I lived in a glass house, literally in a glass house, a house designed by my husband, and I immersed myself in work. I worked alone, I lived apart. I painted the sea in all its moods, and they were my moods, too. The sea was my mirror. I painted the sea in solitude—until I realized that to paint the sea *now* is . . . political. And if I were to paint the sea today, I would paint it as a self-portrait of my body—the new cells in the ocean of my belly roiling, chalk white, little surfaces stippled like old shells, strands of plastic waving around the dividing zygote like kelp—a dying constellation of cells in a dying ocean on a dying planet.

I thought I was as barren as the Earth may someday be. In some ancient cultures, a woman was considered complete when her month blood soiled her thighs. She painted her body, then, fecund, stepped outside her family circle and into a circle of drums and voices, choosing a mate, choosing to have children, choosing the living. I got close—I chose desire, I chose a mate, and I chose to want a child, but that child was denied to me, all those years. Now, with cells conjoined in a rash and quick act in the cold wind, at the border of the ocean; now with an ocean in my belly, now what do I choose?

I don't know what I will choose to do. Each morning now, with an ocean in my belly, nauseous, I gag, I throw up. I wish I could lean my head against my easel and weep, but I hardly know what I'm beginning to feel. This I know: it's a good thing I have a choice. If the law didn't allow for choice, if I had to submit . . . I watch my right hand tremble and my left hand reach over to clasp it—*calm down.* The paintbrush clatters to the floor. I don't have to submit, it's my decision, I tell myself. My body. My pain. My choice. My self-respect. And my self-respect whispers, *Rest in vividness: inquire, the way you paint. Just do that.*

LENA

I don't know why she no longer comes to see me every day, bringing a drawing pad
  and charcoal.

I don't know why she no longer sits by my bed,

why she no longer watches the river with me.

But she said, earlier she said, I heard her say she wants to draw me.

And I said, Fine, that's fine.
                              Draw me without boundaries.

When she was here with me, drawing, I could watch her waist thicken.

She didn't tell me why her waist was thickening,
but that was the way I told time.

It still is.

I can still see her waist thicken. I watch her hand moving quick
across the stiff paper.

She is showing, if barely, but she will not show me. Ha! Ha!

"Not yet," she said. When it's complete . . . not until then, Amma."

That's what she said.

And now this morning, look, oh look, there is a window, its frame and glass
splashed with sunlight,

and it is floating on the river, turning a little in the swirling,
the sunlit window
of my mother's bedroom, and I am little.

My mother. My mother mother mother. Who could resist her?
So long ago now,
                I am still in her bedroom—

I remember the hems of the curtains stirring in the open window.

She liked to nap in the afternoon, and she would tell me things.

Before I had you, there were others, she said.
There was so much blood,
                she said.

I was too young too young too young, wasn't I too young to hear it,

so much blood. It was too early
too early,
          the rug at her feet was red,

she said she said she said, and it is not important, that red,

although the red rug
had a mouth
and the red rug

told me, in barely a whisper,
you will never have children.

In the afternoons, she drew me into her arms.

She talked to me so softly, it felt like love.

All that pain, she said, but now . . . here you are.

Here you are,
                    and she left me to nap in her room,
in her bed, near the open window

and I watched
the hems of the curtains lift and fall,

lift and pause, and fall, lift and fall

as if the Earth were breathing with me, for me.

The rug was red, my mother had been in pain in pain
in pain

with me, because of me, she almost died, but here,
I am, yes,
                    breathing . . .

I am still here, there is a river outside my window.

I sit and wait, I breathe in, I breathe out.

I watch the curtains. I can smell the river.

"I won't I won't I won't," I say.

There you go, the woman-shadow says.

"No never," I say.

There now, there there.
                              Don't cry.

INTERVALE

The earth continues.
                    One could say that Gaia is shrugging us off.

One could say that Gaia detects an imbalance in her body and is on the defensive.

One could say that she has decided that human beings are the more deadly virus, and she is sluffing us off before it's too late.

LENA

Now, this morning, she is as calm as the river is. She drinks her tea.

Mist is rising off the river,
and she doesn't see it yet, slowly gathering into the solidity of form,

a white long-legged bird on the far bank, wading into the smoking mist,
peering into it.

Yes, I do, I do see it. The world is burning. The world is melting.

Mist rises into the dark pines, the pines seem to float, and on the far bank
unbidden
         the white bird

stalks the possibility of fish. *A great a great a great . . .*

regret, she thinks.

It's a great egret. Common once along the coast and salt marshes,
rare now, come inland looking for food,

with a deft swoop of its neck, the bird seizes a fish in its long beak.

Who could see it coming?

Out of nowhere, unbidden, a fish.

Now it flaps, lying horizontally across the interior of the long beak.

And the bird is still, so still.

Is it stunned? she wonders.

A fish. A life. My life.

She watches, as gradually the bird flips the fish

a quarter of an inch,
              an inch,
                      turning the length of it

so that it may fit, and now it does fit, into the narrow space of the bird's
long beak.
              How canny. It knows no haste.

The bird must be hungry.
                      But not greedy, not grateful, not amazed.

All that would be extra.

And now the fish fits the channel of the long beak, and with a single
shake of its head

the bird transforms the fish into a knot in its long neck.

Even the swallowing is slow. As if the bird needs to get used to it,
the kill.

Well now.

Am I the fish that is eaten
against its will,
                    surely against its will—

or am I the regret
into whose empty mind, biding its time,

comes by surprise
just what it has been waiting for—

so that life—unbidden life—is sustained and multiplied,

and death
            is another life

swallowed into the long birth canal of dying alone alone alone.

ZOE

Before I can decide, I must see. Before I can
see, I must look. Before I can look, I have to close my eyes, right now,

I have to close my eyes and put my finger on the painted labyrinth which hangs on the wall in Amma's study, my studio now. A hanging scroll, made of canvas, painted with composite lines of red and purple and white, it offers a path that winds around and around, coming in close, backing off far, turning right, turning hairpin, turning left, turning until there is no right, no left just going on ahead, looking for the center, where there is a painted heart. It is the labyrinth of mourning and loss, and as I place my finger on the canvas, I follow a path Amma must have traced with her finger years ago after Grampa died. She must have wept, and I want to, but I cannot. I follow the path; the paint, thickly applied and rough with age, guides me. As I follow the path to the center and back out to the entry, I watch my finger as if it were Amma's, as if it were my own, as if it were a compass needle off center, crazed, committed to finding its way. I move my finger, 1 inch along, closing my eyes to glide or to lurch into the dark, finding or losing my way—I can't tell which.

At night, I wake up and walk this house in the dark, no moon to light my way, shunning the lamps I could light but don't. I find my way by touch. I reach out my arms wide, I'm a swan or a great bird, and my wings tip at the touch of a chair's arm, the pointed corner of a chest, and the room reassembles itself, I can see the rug and the table, the line of chairs, the painting of the field Amma loves. I am in the dining room. Or I tip my wings against the hard line of a corner, the soft line of open space: I'm in the hallway, nearing the kitchen, about to avoid a cabinet, about to turn left at the painting of the full-breasted woman and enter the hallway out to the door, out to the yard, where no moon is waiting, where the bench that looks down to the pond is barely visible, and the slope of the old butterfly garden is blotted out. I listen for owl or coyote. I imagine stars—then I blot them out one by one with a thick and caustic kohl-black paint,

                                                        and against that backdrop,
I become my own portrait, my face as white as Munch's screaming woman.
I am the open mouth in the skull of her face. As I howl, I stamp my feet until
the ground I stand on trembles. And when I finish, by dawn-light I return to
the labyrinth of mourning, where I discover that if I move my finger along the
pathway over and over, eyes open or closed,

I understand—you must turn your back on where you want to go. That is labyrinthine wisdom. Sometimes you are farther away when you're closest to; sometimes the only way is roundabout and long. I can't *think* my way. I must follow with my finger on a path painted on canvas. Trial and error, hit or miss, right or wrong, I let the opposites fall away—no *Yes;* no, *Not yet;* and no, *No.* Thinking fades away, and I move my finger silently between the lines, the path like a river, and at last, I begin to cry. Softly at first, like a spring rain. Then the sobbing, my body heaving, until I bend over and put my head in my own lap and wait for the storm to pass. The ocean heaves. Rain stipples the sand, soaks it dark. In the wetlands and marshes, their boundaries shift and widen. Water swirls down a dirt road and off into the woods. My shoulders shake. *Enough,* I whisper to the watershed I am. But I keep on crying,

I keep on, until, lifting my head, I remember moving my entire body around and around the four walls of a museum room, on which had been mounted a portrait-scroll of the Connecticut River, foreshortened in some places, for sure, but the entire course of the river was there. I was traversing miles and miles as I circled the room, circling and circling until I couldn't see to see, and I took a seat on the single bench in the middle of the room. The river flowed around and around me. I was the middle of the river, I was the center of a flowing catapult of waterfall, and I kept moving with the river around snag, alongside city concrete and country field, around fish ladders, shallows, harbors, and eddies.

Each day now, I keep moving,
and each day—so far, so good—I choose to paint. That's the easy decision. I
pretend I am only here in Amma's house, away from the city, away from family,
away from friends, to wait and remember, to let myself weep when I must,
to sweat in the heat, to walk the house at night, to sift through the boxes of
papers Amma has left behind. Older, she grew careless with her papers. "I am
disorganizing my papers," she laughed. Why I'm saving anything of hers, I don't
know. Who will read it? If I burn them, her words will only add more carbon
into the atmosphere beginning to choke with carbon as the dying choke on
their own mucus. As for Amma . . . Oh I can't bear to think of her, so alone, so
apart. I put my charcoal to paper, a soft line, a space . . . then a hard line,

and the charcoal slips from my fingers. If I do, if I *dismiss* this pregnancy, will I have another chance? I am *with child,* yes. And what is the loss of one unborn being to the loss of a species in the snarled net we used to call *Nature?* As for those dying now in the journal that will come to be called the plague years, who can understand why? Does a life that is unborn, waiting at a threshold. count for more than those who are living now, suffering now, complicit and afraid?

Tell me—I speak to no one, I speak to myself—
is it still courageous, or right, to choose . . . life? I would scrape clean every
canvas I've ever painted, scrape each one back to blankness, scrape them
beyond blankness, scrape them back to a primordial transparency . . . if only I
could answer that question . . .

LENA

They call this place of inner mist and absence
"memory care,"
                    but she likes to speak

in rift zones and stars:

There's a sizzle in my bones. Pay attention.

I'd like to go back to the place with the trees,
just to smell it.

She hums into the shadows. Solo, her voice
breaks.
                    Out of silence, she invents a chorus.

When she can, she offers others the help she'd like to have.

Dorcas is looking for a way out?

She opens the door.

Edna's hands are trembling?

She holds them in her own hands, which also tremble.

Silvie is hungry?

She finds a nurse and takes her to Silvie, asleep in her room.

"How do you know she's hungry?" the nurse asks,
returning her to her own room.

Because I am, she thinks.

"Tend to your own needs, stay in your own room," she is told.

She leaves her room, and she enters another's.

Let's play baby bird. I'll put food in your mouth.

Let me sing to you. Let me brush your hair.

Do you feel safe with me?

Do you know what is what is what is the soul?

Is there a soul?

Look here,
              here's

a book of paintings. Yellow fields. Black birds. A woman whose eyelids are green.

Jaune. Noir. Verte.

Mais il y a beaucoup d'oiseaux dans les champs.

But there are many blackbirds in the fields.

Personne ne sort vivant d'ici.
                    No one gets out of here alive.

ZOE

Have you noticed, Amma, that we humans, despite evidence to the contrary, still believe we manage to live according to decisions we make? I speak to you with my back to the mirror where I cannot bear to see myself. I am mad at the world. I am mad at what I can't change. I am angry with our species, and at myself. We think we can live with The Warming. If we can't, we'll colonize outer space. We think we will live, no matter what, no matter who or what we turn away from. This morning I drink my coffee in the rising mist of the pond, in burgeoning and in chaos, and I talk to you—you feel close.

Leafed out fully now, the swamp maple, the oldest and only maple tree left, towers over the browning grass. Is it grateful to be alive? Do its roots reach to the sea? Is it . . . content? Amma, what if I told you that I'm pregnant? *With child* . . . those old-fashioned words. What if I said that a part of me (which part, what is the name of that part, what is its voice, the timbre of its voice, what does it look at, what does it see), what if I said that a part of me is eerily content? If for a moment only, and then I become the only and oldest wolf tree maple left alive, seen by no one, a cubist painting, a maple seen in the thousand-faceted eye of a greenbottle fly hovering over the carcass of the Earth. Oh, Amma, who else can I tell this to, but you?

Amma, I'm reading your journals in bed at night, and in the morning before I go into the studio I've made of your old study. From the south-facing window I can see the pond. The window is small, the light filtered by wing shadow and leaf flutter. The light comes in, east of my easel. I think I should not be reading your journals, but I can't help myself. From the window I see the stone bench, the dry grass, and the Tibetan prayer flags I found in one of the journals and tied to the maple wolf tree. There is an old skeleton of a cedar left, its reddish bark faded to a smooth gray finish. It's as iconic as antlers. I look out on the yard where I did moon dances when I was thirteen on the evening's summer grass, a full moon just clearing the rim of the now long-gone oaks. The yard was in leaf shadow then. My feet were damp. You were laughing, and I whirled and whirled. Laughter and whirling . . . still here. As you, also, are—a presence that makes me feel not so entirely alone.

So long ago, learning to draw, I was told to study a feather. To look, then look again. Then, turn away, and without looking at the feather, draw it. To draw is to reimagine, to summon back into being. And so now, I turn away, toward an elegy of line and shadow, wanting to draw your likeness, Amma, your light.

But for days, I cannot draw her. Now even my dreaming has stopped. Pregnant, *yes*. Barren of images, also *yes*. I read Amma's journals—her words make images, and I feed on them. Otherwise, I'd go blank. One morning, after a bad night, no sleep, I come upon a jumble of words in the journal, some of them crossed out. And then a space, and then this, as out of nowhere, a poem:

If, as we say, it's true
death's our common ground—
whose blood is it sucks upward in the mud
making the small
kissing sounds beneath my shoes
in the winter thaws? And at night why
am I still walking
beneath the banded clouds
that make the slender field look light enough
to hover in the air . . .
never far off the red tail, riding
thermals, in that sharp eye no mist to curtain
the river's polished curve,
the slightest fever stirring in the grass
its target—say, the winged-seed white of a throat,
a woman walking in panic
from years of solitude and dread
as the hawk haunts her bed, her field of blood
our common ground—
if as I say . . .

And then she writes words that make me shiver on this kiln-hot day: *I will be present to dying in a different way. Wordless. Raw. A bare presentation.*

I reread the words until Amma's pain seeps into me, settles, then dissolves and slips away. A time to live, a time to die. I ask myself, doubled—as if looking into a mirror—Can I, in these times, all alone, forsaking all others, give birth to a child? If not, can I in these times, all alone, embracing what is left of this earth, bear to kill a mass of cells that might become a child? I tremble. How will I answer my own questions? I don't trust words; I don't trust that we mean what our words say. But is silence an answer? I don't know. I don't know. I drink coffee. The mist rises. I drink the mist. I drink leaf shadow and sun, and I begin to draw the wolf tree maple, so alive that nothing has killed it yet. And I go outside to walk the labyrinth of deer trails in these woods, where there is, despite die-back, still life.

INTERVALE

For one hundred thousand years this part of the world was covered with tundra and glacial ice, and great mammals roamed the earth.

Luckily, not all the large mammals were lost at the start of the Holocene as homo sapiens fanned out and spread across the continents, hunting.

The glaciers receded, and ten thousand years ago across what is now North America, boreal forests were established. By 3,500 BCE, the forests had become thick with pine, oak, beeches. It was warmer.
Imagine,

in the early forests, outside any flow of time or logic, imagine a journal, its pages riffling in the cold wind. The pages are blank. Anything can happen.
Imagine words.

Words won't be invented or written down for centuries, but let's imagine words: it's only a matter of time before an old woman opens a journal and writes,

What if the Big Bang wasn't the birth of the Universe, but its conception? Conception would imply that we are burgeoning cells in an evolving and present Being. Conception would imply that all there is,
imagine this,

is One Body. That we are not particles blown apart in a vast continuing explosion; we are particles thrown together in a turning, swirling spiral. One body.
Imagine that.

ZOE

        The deer trails begin on the far side of the pond, less distinct among the ferns, and they loop and wind through thickets and glades. Here's a tree stripped by deer of bark in winter, here's an old wolf tree with a low limb that stretches out like a bench—I can sit there for hours counting the needles on the nearby hemlocks, the striations on the shelf fungus on the old stump at my feet. The trails wind through mossy hummocks in patches of wetland, one of them skirts a ledge, where I sniff the air for the scent of cucumbers—a copperhead is said to smell like cucumbers. Coppers like ledges. The trails seem to have no destination; and it is all destination. I float into the silence I inhabit when I am painting. The woods are not silent: but I am,

silent, and therefore, I see more clearly.
Even at night when I follow a deer trail into moonrise and moon arc. Even
when I stumble and cry out. Even when the owl hears me, and sharply answers
back, and I am afraid. Stumbling back to the house, weary of reading the path
with my feet, I stand for who knows how long in front of the mirror in the hall.
Then without a word in my head, I turn myself out of the house and enter the
woods again, footstep by footstep, retracing the trail. The ground turns dusky
and mauve in the morning. The sun is a streak. Stroke by stroke, that's how I
build a painting, until stroke by stroke, an image emerges, the eye perceives it
and knows what it is,

or it doesn't—it doesn't know. Out of the settled house, back onto the winding trail, blocked now by bull briar, thwarted by disappearance, I follow a trail as it lifts into the air, where I can't go, nor can the deer. I follow the pathways between the tree branches birds navigate, leaving no trace. No trace. I stand alongside a glacial erratic. I stand until I feel the glacier move, and I follow . . . what? Instinct? Deeper knowing? I don't know anything for certain, that's what I'm certain of.

And then it happens. A trail spills out of the woods into a field so bright yellow it hurts my eyes. It must be noon. No shadows, except those beneath the cedars. The stone walls glitter. The ridgeline beyond the field is green. There is, for a moment, the stillness of arrival. A storm's coming, I'm out in the open, exposed, struck still, and wildly happy, without knowing why.

Not long after finding myself in the yellow field, I awaken slowly, exactly as if I'd fallen from a plane of color, migratory mauve and green carried by the least wind into a world of form and solidity and shadow, and the colors turn slowly, as if on an axis, then settle over an open space. The space is gold, and it lifts, as water and light lift, rising above the ground. *Child, little no one as yet come into the sunlight, I will not refuse you a body.* That sentence, made without me, arrives complete in my mind. A sentence made without me, but through me, then delivered intact, just as my eyes open on morning sky. That sentence might be the title of a painting emerging in my mind, but it rings like a decision I can trust with my life, and it *is* my life, even though the Earth may not survive long enough for my child to grow old, nor may I, who knows? Or we may live long, only to forget and be forgotten. Time passes, I don't know how much time, disguised as space, passes, but I have been waking up, these hot spring mornings, keeping my vow of silence, squinting toward the windows whose upright and transverse mullions divide the surface into rectangles—

the world is a painting, multiple paintings, waiting to be seen. A life is multiple also, waiting to be lived. What I sense beyond or through the window-glass beckons. It conjures me. I stay there in bed a while, and when I open my eyes more fully, depth is restored, solidity is restored. The names of things cry out from their bounded spaces, and I can see the mirror over the dark-wood dresser as it reflects the white walls opposite. I stand up. I stand before it, a singularity I once called *myself*. No more. I am present. I am plural. I put my hand on the little rise of my belly. *Parce que je suis ici, nous sommes ici.* Because I am here, we are here.

To celebrate, I have taken outdoors all the hanging mirrors in the house—there are five of them—and I have hung them on the clapboards of Amma's house. The mirrors face the woods, gathering them in wind or in stillness. Mirror is now an invitation that reflects what remains of the luminous, the living world. Amma said to me once, *Look! Want to see? Want to see the world more fully?* We were floating in the pond, and when I looked more closely, I saw we were also floating in a towering cloud that by late afternoon might bring thunder, but which now was temporarily snagged on a reach of pine branch, on which I also floated. I saw water skimmers zoom and zigzag. I saw blue dragonflies touch and go on the surface of what I now knew hid invisible supernovas.

Because of COVID and seclusion, I haven't been to see Amma. Now she has for company only her memories. Perhaps not even those. My walking the deer trail labyrinth in the woods and wetlands has taken me away from her and brought me also closer. When I think of her, I slip into her silences, crossing a boundary that shifts and settles, then shifts again. I never know when I am in danger of slipping deeper in—Amma is, at times, an ocean. At times I can't tell my thoughts from hers. (I still think she's able to have thoughts). So that it may be just as well that I am with her only by proxy, only by being in her house, on her land, finding my way by losing it. I want to be sure my decision to have you, little no one as yet, is entirely mine.

I still keep a vow of silence. Each morning, I leave Amma's house, walking out only into the woods, into the shrinking wetlands, whose borders shift with each rainfall. I practice getting lost. I revisit the field I didn't know I'd find. I breathe it in. I practice finding my way home. I swim in the pond. Now that I have hung the mirrors on the clapboards, coming home I catch a flash of myself among a collage of shagbarks and bare oaks and stars and wind-blur. I do not stand out. I am not separate. I can no longer say, "I love my body" without meaning the body that is mine and not mine; the body that is not one, not two; the body whose borders shift with each footfall. And the moon? The moon is a flower in my hair.

Child, little no one as yet come into the sunlight, I will not refuse you a body or a mind. You will be who you will be. I will be a single mother. I will not have a steady income. I cannot educate you as I have been educated, feed you as I have been fed, clothe you as I have been clothed. As you grow older, sunlight will tarnish your skin. The rain will singe it. There is no way to shelter you from the torque of winds. I do not have health insurance, fire insurance, flood insurance, food insurance, memory insurance. There are no assurances, only assays on your own in the land of the never-free-enough, where only the rich are free, and if you're poor, it's your fault. I give you to the universe for safe keeping.

Oh, and the moon is not a flower in my hair.
Whoever said that was . . . giddy. No. The moon and I float in one pond here
together. And in that place, there is no birth, no death—only conception and
continuation. I can live with that. This morning once again I felt you, little one
soon to enter the sunlight; I felt you stir in my body. There is an ocean in my
belly. You swim there.

     Who knew?

INTERVALE

It is not difficult to tell when one is dying.

The light around the body changes.

The look in the eye changes; in some, a faraway look. In others, a presence never there before.

Breathing changes, becomes color around the body's mist.

For all of us on Earth, it's time to notice that the sea, the sea is moving closer.

For those who know how to see it, the light that pulses around the body of the Earth is also changing.

Take a breath.

LENA

Last will and testament. It's time for that.

I do not, of course, believe in heaven.
I believe in the Earth
and its small raptures.

Zoe Zoe Zoe, as I leave you,

I leave you
            a window in winter-bonfire sunlight,

red trumpets flaring, blossoms coming into light and time,

into themselves—amaryllis.

I look out the window into a morning the color of daybreak
on a day it will rain,

and someone in a small boat is rowing rowing rowing—

heart pump, an ache in the arm muscles,
steady breath.

The wake the wake the wake unfurls and widens.

Gather me. I will pay the boatman, but not with a coin—

I will pay the boatman with a moment of amaryllis.

With a glimpse of a mountain
seen through stalks of hay on a steep field.

With the prayer wheel that has turned and turned
within me all these years.

Once we came back into the house in a wind-drift of petals
from the wild cherry tree,

petals in our hair.

I will pay the boatman a wind-drift of petals,

a coin of sun on the rumple of our clothes
at the foot of the bed.

I will offer up dove call,
the cat purring in the bend of my body,

night stars in the bare uplift of tree branches.

Light rises, it travels the mind,
it becomes time,
                becomes

the hem of a curtain lifting and falling
in a window barely left open,

becomes the red rug, even that,
it becomes
            the sun

not yet rounding through the black branches,
becomes
            breathing hard after sex,

becomes walking over the crest of the hill
wind-blown
                into a field of sunlit grass . . .

Dear Zoe, the boatman has come to the river beyond my window,

and I know you will come to look at me one last time.

The door is open.

Wherever you are, look back at me . . .

Or better better better yet, come today.

Come again tomorrow.
                                        Reviens demain.

Now she sleeps, now

she dreams of her granddaughter, standing at the threshold of her room
a long moment
                    taking her in.

We are taking each other in. The light around your belly
is no longer amethyst and blue,

it is the color
                    of the roses

I put into a row of small vases on a strip of mirror
along a polished table,
                    a doubled blooming.

Oh, I came so near to it, that doubled blooming.

ZOE

As I draw, I can't see her. She is in Room 19. (*I'm at your house, Amma. Je suis chez toi.*) I can't see the back of her head as it rests against the pillow. Of course, I can remember having seen the back of Amma's head—perhaps she was reading a book, taking notes, her silver hair held in a silver clip. Or perhaps I came up behind her as she leaned her head on Grampa's shoulder when he could no longer say words. And because I remember, as I sit by the bed and draw her portrait, I imagine there is a back to her head, a closure to the openness of her gazing out the window to the river. It is the same way with a vase. One assumes the back of it is there when all one really sees is the front.

But what if the back of Amma's head were as open as the sky? What if, behind what I can see of her face and thinning hair and large ears, there is only vast expanse, a sky crowded with stars, a field of stars that swirl, come into being, intensities of flame passing through the light and distance of space time, utterly un-knowable. No wonder night sky made Pascal wonder why he had been born in this pocket of vast expanse, why this time is the time allotted him to live. No wonder he was terrified. Why am I here? he asked, as I ask myself now, wanting to be beside Amma's bed, wanting her near me. *Draw me without boundaries,* she said.

I remember, and I draw. Or I hold the charcoal in abeyance, almost touching the paper, and I don't move. At times, drawing her, the intensity is so great I believe the charcoal will burst into flame and consume us both. While I draw Amma, or grow more ready to draw her without boundaries, a humming rises in the back of the mind. Don't go back to sleep, the humming inside me says. Again, I slip inside the charcoal, slip into Amma and into the humming that comes from us both . . . It took an ocean and desire and a body in tidal impact to begin the cellular union my body now cradles. But it takes presence and love to receive the miracle of acceptance. And so, I draw.

LENA

Where did the river the river the river begin?

She says the words aloud to the empty room,
actual words,

she says them, then remembers how she balanced
on her knees

in the deep shade beyond the sunlit field—
was she praying?

Even now she can feel it, the damp earth . . .

And I knew I was I was I was
as now: I was at the source
of an upwelling,
                              clear water
that would gather and run downhill,
becoming brook, becoming river,
and I knelt, I tried to hold
the upwelling water in my hands,
to collect and keep it,
                              but I couldn't
I couldn't: no, I couldn't hold it.

I could only drink it, I could only
try to take it in, my whole weight
pressing into the earth
as I drank what I could, as I
drank what little I was given,
the rest of it
                    running running running
through my fingers . . .

And then she sleeps, without dreams, for hours.

ZOE

At the window of Room 19, with sun and the shadow from the maple tree on the glass, I look in, my hands on the curve of my body, just where my child is kicking, little flutter kicks. I see that the head of the bed is raised slightly. Amma is in silhouette against the bright window, in a corner of which the river behind me flashes. Tree branches also reflect on the glass that protects the photograph of the field she loves. Shadows move swiftly across the field where Amma once stood, waiting. "If you stand still long enough," Amma told me once, "you may see mountains move."

I'm outside the window glass, looking in. I cannot enter the room, put down my things, or settle myself on the edge of her bed. Her face is in the light now—her eyelids flutter when I murmur, "I'm here with you, Amma." Her eyes do not open. Her hands must feel cold to touch, even on this sultry day. I take my hands and place them onto the swelling of my belly, and I hold them gently there.

With my hands on my belly, holding them gently there, I wonder if she might be awake enough, if she will know how to touch at a distance, or whether I should speak. Her eyelids flutter open, and her eyes meet mine, and when they do, I am stunned into recognition. Her whole body gives out light. The river, it must be a flash of sun from the river, I think, a flickering off the mirror of the window glass. But no. She is the source, I am certain of it, as if a tidal surge of light swept upward toward the shore, shattered into gold flecks, then pulled back. Back under. There's a river in her wrist. There's an ocean in my belly. There's a field of light around us.

I imagine Amma's hands on my belly. The moment is too precious to spoil with words. We do not move. My hands on my belly are her hands, my hands warm hers. We are a still life. Her eyes close, open, close. Somewhere an ocean rolls and wind whips white crescents into the surface. I withdraw my hands from hers, from my belly. From a large folder I take out the charcoal and watercolor drawing I've made for her. Her eyes open, and she watches me show her the pond becoming sky, the sky becoming pond, a succession of mirrors into which the ten thousand things come forward like ripples in the stillness, and as they come forward, they do not disturb the stillness.

Drawn in charcoal, barely visible, Amma is there, her profile a skein of geese emerging from a cloud on the skin of the pond.

On the window glass between us, light paints what is present. We are, each of us, a reverse glass painting of the other, for the other, because of the other. Amma's face rises in a skein of geese, the geese fly through the maple leaves, the leaves flutter on the bedspread, on the glass of the photograph of the field, and the field is a ripple of air, an ocean of sunlight, and then—am I dreaming this? her hands, reaching for what I have drawn,

come to rest on my belly.
If we are waiting for the child to stir, we don't have to wait long. Amma smiles. She nods, her eyes still holding mine. Her hands shift slightly. They rub my belly, light as brushstrokes. Her eyes close. I don't know how much time passes or if it passes. Amma opens her eyes again, and I don't want to go from this moment. It is like the sun. It is like the moon. It is like darkness. Anything can happen.

LENA

I wish I could tell you how beautiful this is

Over the river, an opening

                    And there is light, there is light

the color of daybreak

The sea moves closer

                    The sea moves closer to the sun, also, the field

Oh, look into my eyes

                    See for yourself, the one shining field

this once, this once

                    this everlasting and only once

THIS BOOK IS DEDICATED TO ELLEN WILLIAMS KYMPTON

I would like to thank early readers of this book for their encouragement: Edwina Trentham and other members of the Connecticut River Poets. More recent readers offered generous and cogent suggestions, and I thank them in particular. This book, and my life, would not be the same without you: John Long, Arlene Scully, and Chase Twichell.

I am grateful to Pamela Zagarenski for her permission to let her painting, "The Spiral Path," be the cover of this book. Imagination knows no boundaries.

The labyrinth along which Zoe runs her finger was painted by Gregory Coleman.

The portrait-scroll of the Connecticut River was painted by Charles Chu and exhibited in the Lyman Allyn Museum in New London, CT.

There are echoes of two writers: Rebecca Solnit (page 15) and Barbara Hurd (page 30). If there are other echoes, I make a deep bow to their sources as well.

My gratitude to those who looked over and corrected my French: Leigh Ranucci and Neal Novak.

The poem in Lena's journal appeared first as "Compline" in *Icon and Evidence* by Margaret Gibson, LSU Press, 2001.

Printed in the USA
CPSIA information can be obtained
at www.ICGtesting.com
CBHW032320181124
17629CB00031B/624